A *FIRST BOOK* OF ANIMALS

by
Margaret Crush

Piccolo
A Piper Book

Contents

Graham Allen

The Animal Story

From the blue whale, the largest of all living things, to the tiniest insect; from the fastest cheetah streaking through the jungle to the slow tortoise crawling in your garden—all these are part of the animal kingdom. But hundreds of millions of years ago, the only living things were some tiny blobs of floating jelly that lived in the sea.

How then did we get all the different animals that we know today? Many scientists believe that they all grew from these first blobs of jelly.

After a long period of time, the specks of jelly began to change shape. Some turned into animals such as sponges and jellyfish. And some of these sponge-like creatures developed into worms, snails and fish.

All these animals lived in the sea. But eventually some fish discovered that life could be easier close to the water's edge, where there were plenty of plants and insects to eat. These fish crawled out of the water and became amphibians. Amphibians are animals which can live both in water and on land, like frogs and newts today.

Millions of years later, another great change took place. Some amphibians developed into reptiles, such as snakes and lizards. The first important group of reptiles were the great dinosaurs.

For 150 million years, reptiles dominated the Earth. Huge dinosaurs lumbered over the land. Sea serpents squirmed through the seas. And flying reptiles glided through the skies.

Some small reptiles grew feathers to keep warm. In time, their limbs became wings, and the first birds took to the skies.

The first reptiles were small, sharp-toothed beasts with short legs. Later there were reptiles with longer legs, like the one below. All the dinosaurs may have descended from this type of reptile.

Other reptiles developed into the first mammals. These were probably tiny, and ate only insects. But when the great dinosaurs began to die out, the little mammals no longer had to lurk under bushes in terror of the fierce meat-eating giants. They ventured timidly into the open and made their homes in new places. Some, like the ancestors of monkeys, lived in trees. Others lived in the sea, like whales and dolphins today. These look like fish, but because their young are born alive and suck milk from their mother, they are mammals. Fish, reptiles and amphibians all lay eggs.

Mammals grew bigger, because now they could find food other than insects to eat. Some began to eat plants, and others fed off other animals.

In time, all the 4000 different mammals we know today had appeared. There were cats, dogs, bears, mice, apes and monkeys— and even the first people!

But the Earth was also changing. About two million years ago the winters became colder and the summers shorter. The world was entering an Ice Age.

Many animals could not adapt to the bitter cold. Some, like elephants, hyenas and cheetahs, moved south where the weather was warmer. They left the northern pine forests to the bush-antlered deer and the fierce scimitar cat.

Enormous sheets of ice, called glaciers, crept across Europe and North America. Sturdy creatures such as woolly mammoths and bison roamed the edges of the glaciers in search of food.

As the Ice Age came to an end, the glaciers melted. Many creatures, such as polar bears and seals, had become so used to the cold that they moved north where there was still much ice and snow. But many other animals died out altogether.

Woolly mammoth

Bush-antlered deer

Scimitar cat

Animal Homes

Some animals, like the bison in the picture, have no real home. They wander in herds across grassy plains, searching endlessly for food. They sleep wherever they happen to stop.

But many animals and insects do build homes. If the home is well protected, with plenty of food and water, a lot of animals may live together.

The picture below shows a prairie dog 'town' in North America. It is made up of hundreds of kilometres of underground tunnels, and many families of prairie dogs live there.

A sentry keeps watch from a mound of soil for enemies. When they hear its warning bark, all the dogs will disappear underground in seconds. But if the visitor is recognized as a member of the family, the sentry will go up to it and greet it.

Bison

Prairie dogs

9

Ruby-throated hummingbird

Golden oriole

Long-tailed tit

Woodpecker

Tailorbird

The Nest Builders

If you see a bird in spring carrying something in its beak, this usually means that it is busy making a nest or feeding its fledglings (baby birds). Sometimes the parent birds build the nest together, but often all the hard work is done by only one.

Some birds are specially clever at building nests. The Asian tailor bird uses its beak as a needle, and sews leaves together to make a swinging cradle for its chicks. The weaver-bird weaves a wonderful hanging nest, while the woodpecker builds a house by drilling a hole in a tree trunk with its beak.

Sand martin

Plover

Wren

A weaverbird builds a nest

Many birds build cup-shaped nests, like the hummingbird and the golden oriole. The tiny wren and the long-tailed tit build a ball-shaped nest, with an entrance hole so small you would never think they could squeeze through! The bowl-shaped nest behind the tailor bird is a familiar sight in most gardens. This type of nest is usually the home of finches, thrushes and blackbirds.

The bittern makes its home among the reeds at the edge of marshes. The pheasant and the plover lay their eggs on the ground.

They have to take special care to protect their young from enemies. The ringed plover will cleverly lure a fox away from its nest by pretending that it has a broken wing. The fox thinks the plover is an easy meal until it suddenly flies away!

But many enemies still find and destroy nests and fledglings. Some birds, like sand martins and kingfishers, think an underground burrow is a far safer place to nest.

Bittern

Pheasant

11

Life Underground

Many animals live underground, where they are safe from enemies and protected from the cold.

A rabbit warren is a maze of rambling tunnels, which is added to over the years by many families of rabbits. A doe (female rabbit) also digs a special burrow, called a stop, for her babies.

The bee builds wax cells for her eggs in a small hole—perhaps an old mouse hole.

A badger's home is known as a sett. Different badgers may use the same home, so a sett can be over a hundred years old. Badgers are very houseproud and keep their setts very clean. They take their bedding outside to air, and they dig special lavatory pits away from the sett. Sometimes a fox will take over an old badger sett, but it is not a tidy owner.

Sometimes you may see mounds of earth called molehills. Moles dig tunnels with their strong front feet, pushing the loose soil away with their back feet.

Slugs lurk in their moist underground homes during the day, so that the sun does not dry them up. Earthworms dig their burrows by swallowing the soil.

Fox

Rabbit

Badger

Mole

Slug

Earthworm

Bumblebee

Garden spider

Comma butterfly

Leaf miner

Gall

Fairy lamp

In the Garden

If you look carefully, you can find all sorts of animals in your garden.

Turn over any large stones or an old piece of rotting wood, and out will scuttle an army of small insects. Woodlice cluster there in huge family groups. The wood may be covered in tiny holes, made by the wood beetle and its grubs. Or you may find earwigs, or the many-legged creatures called centipedes and millipedes.

You may see sunlight glinting across the dewy web made by a garden spider. Sometimes you can spot its egg nursery—a little ball of silk called a fairy lamp.

Maybe you will find a little woody lump on a bramble bush. This is a gall, the nursery of a young grub called a larva. Later, the larva will hatch into a grown insect.

Wiggly lines in leaves might be the work of the tiny leaf miner, the grub of a moth. It burrows into the leaf just as a coal miner digs tunnels in the ground.

Most insects go through several stages to grow into adults. The red admiral butterfly starts life as an egg laid on a plant. The egg

Ant

hatches into a larva (a butterfly larva is called a caterpillar). Many weeks later, the caterpillar spins a hard protective covering known as a chrysalis around itself, and finally it bursts out as an adult insect. Many adult insects have wings, but few are as beautiful as the butterfly's.

If you keep very quiet late in the evening, you might see a hedgehog ambling round your garden. If you leave a saucer of milk out for him he should become a regular visitor. He will earn his keep by eating up the slugs which attack your plants.

A pair of house martins may build their nest in the roof of your house. If they are not disturbed, they will return year after year.

Wood beetle and grub

House martin

Crane-fly

Red admiral

Hedgehog

Chrysalis

Caterpillar

Millipede

Garden snail

Centipede

Woodlouse

The Beehive

Honeybees live and work in huge groups, or colonies. Each colony has one queen bee, about 1000 drones and 50,000 workers. The queen bee spends most of her time laying eggs, and may produce as many as 2000 in one day!

Drones are male bees whose only purpose is to mate with the queen to produce eggs. All the work is done by the female worker bees. They busily build the honeycombs from wax made by their bodies. The honeycombs are split up into small compartments or cells. Into some of the cells the queen lays her eggs, which hatch into grubs.

Beehive

Grubs

Worker bees

Eggs

Grub

Pupa

Young bee

Some bees still nest in the wild

Nursemaid workers look after them, as they change from a grub to a pupa (like a chrysalis) to a bee.

Other workers make thousands of journeys to collect the powdery yellow pollen and sweet nectar from flowers. They carry the pollen in 'baskets' on their legs. Back at the hive, the pollen is made into honey and stored in other cells. When a bee finds a lot of pollen it returns to the hive and dances in the air above it. This dance tells the other bees which direction to go in to find the flowers. Some workers stand at the hive entrance and fan their wings. This keeps fresh air moving around inside the hive. And guard bees protect the hive from enemies.

Bees carry pollen from flower to flower. This helps the flowers to make seeds.

Pollen basket

Ovenbird

Elf owl

Water spider

Mouth breeder

18

Unusual Homes

Some animals live in strange homes.

The small elf owl lives in the desert, and makes its home inside a giant cactus plant. The ovenbird's clay nest looks like an old-fashioned baker's oven, and the potter wasp also builds a little clay nest for its single egg.

The mouthbreeder fish carries its eggs and young in its mouth. The water spider lives in an air bubble underwater, while the tree frog makes a clay-walled nursery.

The ant lion below digs a clever trap, and eats the ants that fall in.

Potter wasp

Brazilian tree frog

Ant lion

The Master Builder

The cleverest engineer in the animal world is related to the white mice we keep as pets. This large rodent is the North American beaver. He is expert at cutting down trees, making dams, and digging canals—all to build

Beavers use the little finger on each hand like a human thumb, to get a firm grip on sticks and branches.

Dam of logs stuck together with clay and leaves.

his splendid island home, called a lodge.

His main tools are his sharp teeth and strong claws. Rodents are gnawing mammals with large chisel-like front teeth. The teeth are covered with very hard enamel. A beaver can chew through a tree 15 centimetres across in just three minutes!

Beaver families work together to build lodges and repair dams. The lodge is always in the middle of a pond or a lake. If there isn't one there already, the beaver will build a dam across a stream or small river to make one!

A single dam may need hundreds of tonnes of wood. Beavers gnaw the trees so that they fall towards the water. If there are no trees near the water's edge, the beaver will dig a canal to the nearest trees.

The beavers carefully cut the trees into pieces they can manage, and float them one by one into position. In the middle of the pool they make their domed lodge. They store lots of juicy shoots and bark there to eat during the long cold winter.

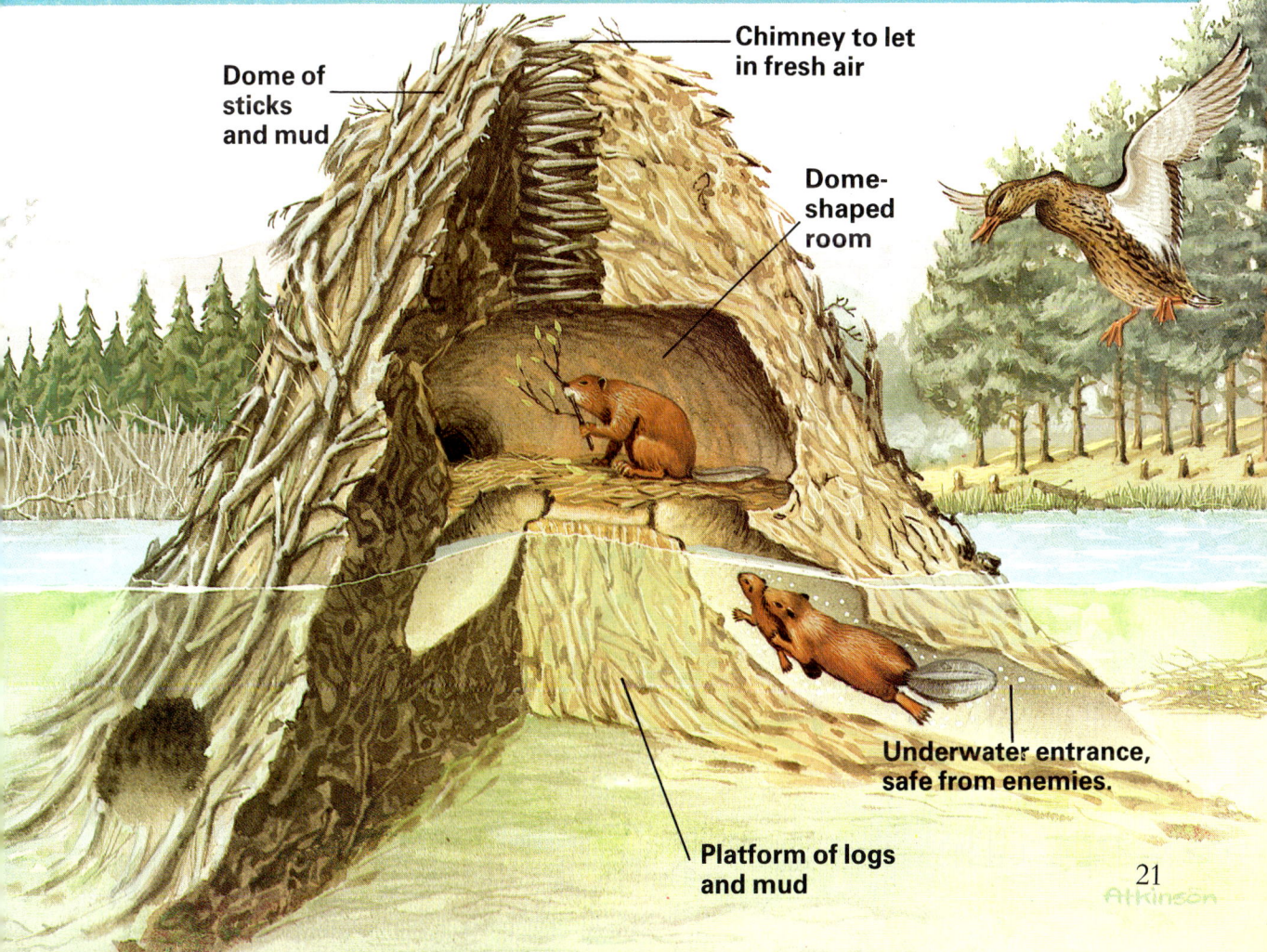

Dome of sticks and mud

Chimney to let in fresh air

Dome-shaped room

Underwater entrance, safe from enemies.

Platform of logs and mud

21

Reed warbler

Kingfisher

Geese

Great crested grebe

Teal

Frog

Dragonfly

Ramshorn snail

Snail eggs

Graham Allen

Pond Life

A pond is alive with animals. Insects and birds swim above it. Pond skaters and whirligig beetles skim across its surface. Frogs hop from one lilypad to the next. And many different fishes and newts swim under the water.

A dazzling blue-and-orange kingfisher swoops down and pulls out a fish. A glittering dragonfly flashes by, grabbing at insects with its legs.

The dragonfly's grub (called a nymph) lives underwater. It feeds off insects and fishes often larger than itself. The great diving beetle is a fierce hunter, too.

A pond is a nursery for many animals. The grubs (larvae) of mosquitoes zigzag about in the water. Later they will grow wings and fly away. Frogs and toads lay their eggs (called spawn) in the water. These will hatch into black tadpoles. Many water birds tuck their nests away in the reeds, well hidden from danger. Most baby birds have no feathers, and have to be looked after by their parents. But young water birds like ducks can usually swim and feed themselves as soon as they hatch from the eggs.

The male stickleback builds a tunnel nest of pondweed. His mate will lay her eggs there. Then he will carefully guard the nest.

Caddis worms build themselves a suit of armour out of sand or twigs and leaves. They may also weave a net to trap food.

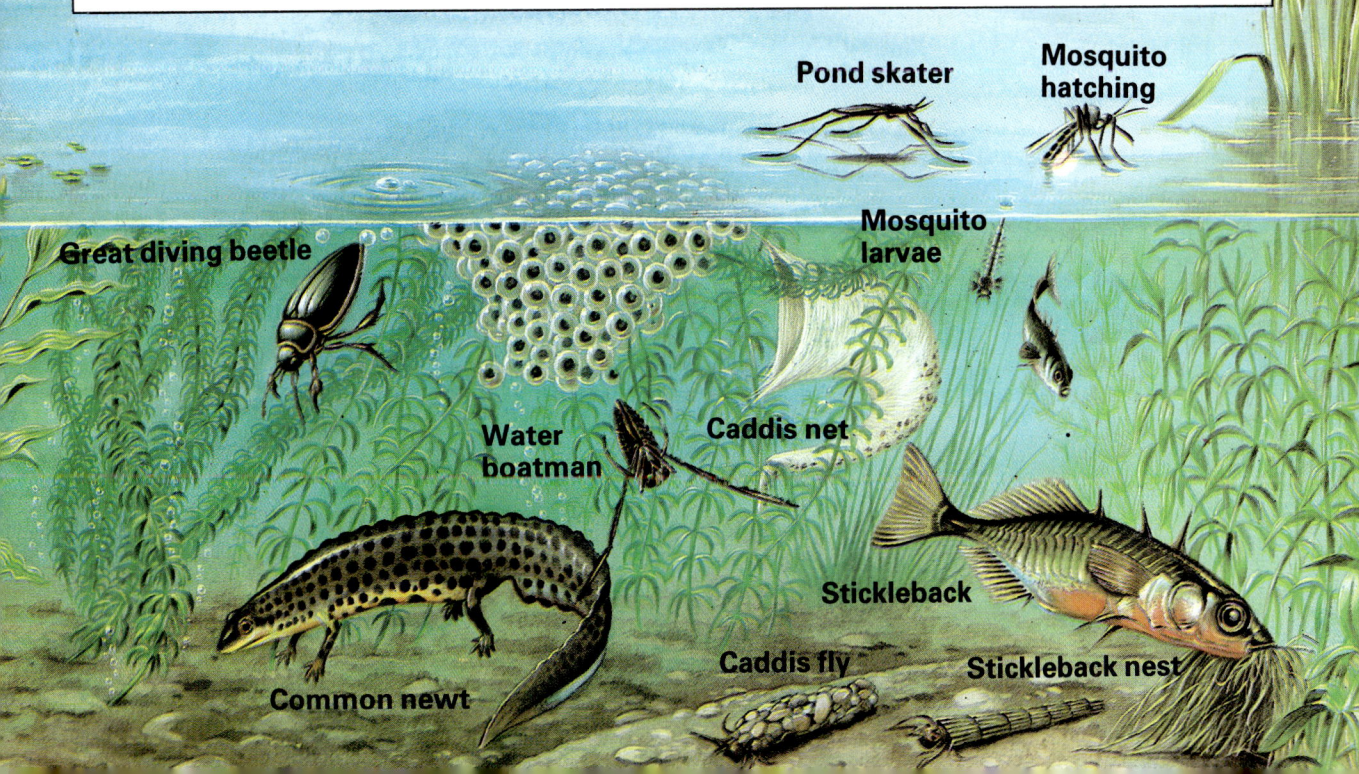

Pond skater

Mosquito hatching

Great diving beetle

Mosquito larvae

Water boatman

Caddis net

Stickleback

Common newt

Caddis fly

Stickleback nest

On the Seashore

If you walk along the seashore, you will find many seashells clinging to the rocks. Some of the most common belong to mussels, barnacles and limpets, all of which wear tough outer shells. The shells protect their soft bodies from drying up when the tide goes out. When the tide is in, these shelled creatures, called molluscs, glide about in search of food.

All seashore life must be able to survive salt water. If they live on a part of the beach that is covered at high tide, they have to put up with being swamped by the sea twice a day. For the rest of the time they are baked by hot sun, blown by cold winds or drenched with rain.

No wonder many sea animals like lugworms burrow quickly into the sand or mud when the tide goes out. If you want to find these animals, you must dig near the low water mark at low tide. But don't waste time looking along a shingle beach. Most animals find that the shifting pebbles make it far too dangerous to live there.

You'll have to dig furiously to catch a burrowing razor shell. It is

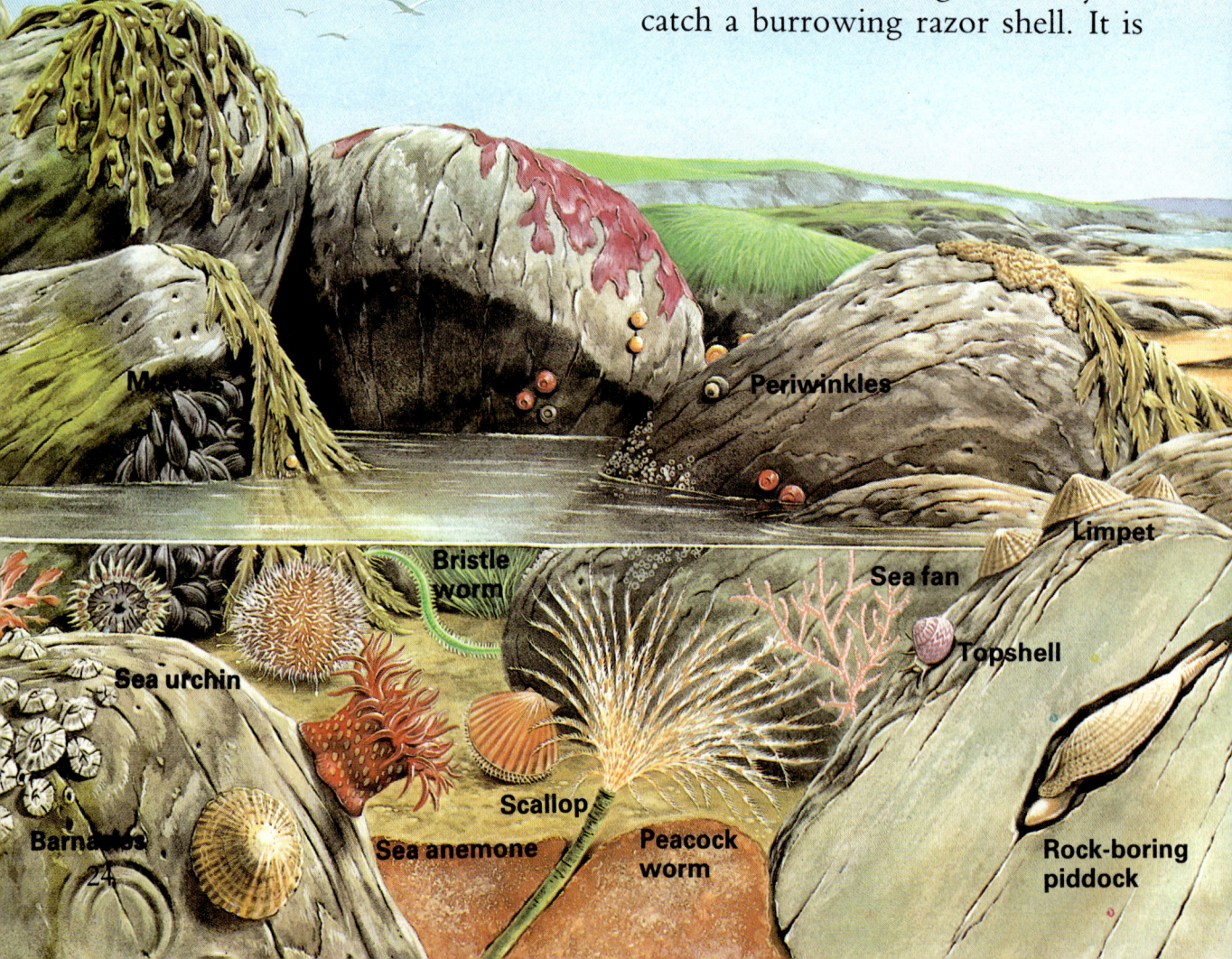

Mussels · Periwinkles · Limpet · Bristle worm · Sea fan · Sea urchin · Topshell · Barnacles · Scallop · Sea anemone · Peacock worm · Rock-boring piddock

so speedy that you will seldom beat it to its lair. You will probably never see one alive, though you may find the empty shell of a dead one.

Seabirds, crabs, sea urchins and many other creatures live and feed on the seashore. When the tide goes out, shrimps, prawns, hermit crabs and small lobsters shelter in the rock pools left behind by the sea.

Although an anemone is a flower, the beautiful sea anemone is an animal. Like the peacock worm, it waves its many arms (tentacles) about to catch small fish to eat. The sea cucumber is also an animal, not a plant. It is a relative of the starfish. Both are found in rock pools, as well as in the sand.

The common tern nests in a hollow on the shore. Many birds that nest on beaches lay patterned eggs to blend with the sand or stones.

The eider duck builds a nest of seaweed, moss and twigs on the shore. It covers its eggs with its soft downy feathers. The word 'eiderdown' comes from this.

Worm casts

Starfish

Whelk

Whelk egg cases

Otter shell

Tellin

Sea-cucumber

Common cockle

Parchment worm

Razor shell

25

Living in the Sea

Many fascinating animals live in the sea itself. One of them is the largest animal that has ever lived—the blue whale. This whale can weigh as much as thirty elephants, but in spite of its size it is very gentle.

The oceans cover almost three-quarters of the Earth's surface. Yet we know very little about them, except for the shallow waters around the land. Here the sea is warm and sunlit, so many more underwater plants like seaweed and plankton can grow. These provide plenty of food for plant-eating sea animals. And these animals make a meal for other animals that feed on them!

Animal plankton

Chemicals rise from the sea-bed

Herring

Shark

Skate

M. CAMM

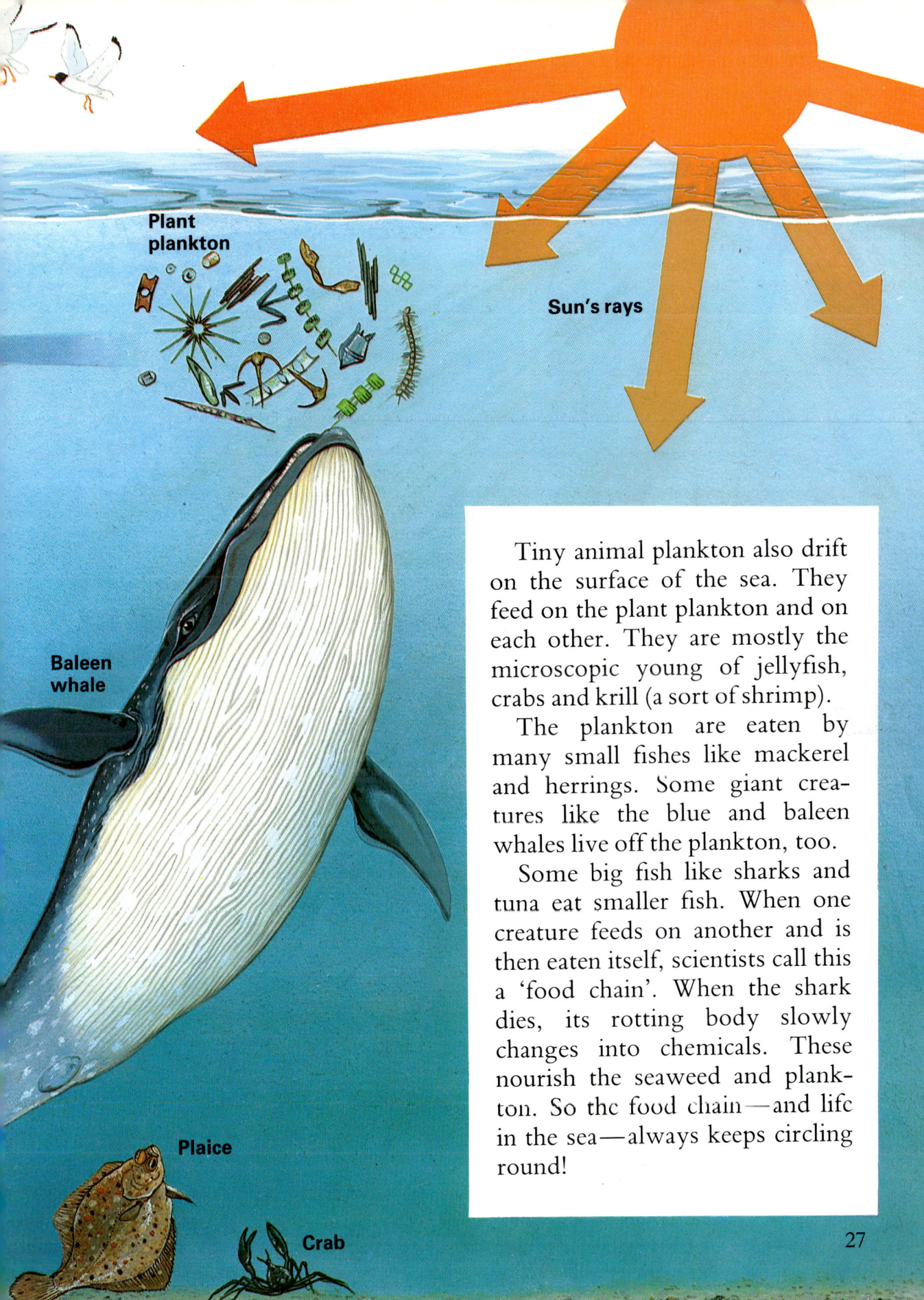

Plant plankton

Sun's rays

Baleen whale

Plaice

Crab

Tiny animal plankton also drift on the surface of the sea. They feed on the plant plankton and on each other. They are mostly the microscopic young of jellyfish, crabs and krill (a sort of shrimp).

The plankton are eaten by many small fishes like mackerel and herrings. Some giant creatures like the blue and baleen whales live off the plankton, too.

Some big fish like sharks and tuna eat smaller fish. When one creature feeds on another and is then eaten itself, scientists call this a 'food chain'. When the shark dies, its rotting body slowly changes into chemicals. These nourish the seaweed and plankton. So the food chain—and life in the sea—always keeps circling round!

The Darkest Deep

In the deepest part of the ocean live some of the strangest-looking creatures in the animal world.

No sunlight reaches these ocean depths. Here there are no plants—and very little food. The fearsome fish that live here cannot afford to miss any meal that happens to swim by. They have huge gaping jaws, and can swallow creatures much bigger than themselves.

Some of the fish in this gloomy deep actually carry their own lighting! Parts of their bodies can be made to glow. The light attracts a mate or a meal, or just confuses their enemies. Some even trail a fishing line with lights on the end, to lure their prey towards them.

Animal Partners

Many animals live on their own, except when they meet for mating. But other animals have discovered that it can be useful to stay together.

Some animals share nursery duties. Female elephants, for example, will look after a group of baby elephants while others feed. A new-born baby whale must reach the surface of the sea quickly, because whales need to breathe air. Female 'midwife' whales help the mother to push the baby upwards, so that it doesn't drown.

Some animals share their homes. A starling may even build its nest on the rim of a huge eagle's eyrie. The starling's enemies may think twice about approaching the bigger bird's nest, and if an intruder *does* approach, the starling's squawk will let the eagle know its nest is in danger.

A sea anemone often sticks itself to the shell of a hermit crab. As the

Oxpecker birds peck at the ticks which irritate the rhinoceros' skin. Below, egrets wait for insects to be stirred up by the animal's hooves. Both birds warn the rhino of approaching danger, by flying away.

crab scuttles about, the anemone enjoys a free ride. It can catch extra supplies of food in its waving tentacles. The hermit crab itself lives in the empty shell of a dead sea snail, where its soft body is protected from enemies.

The African honeyguide bird will lead the honey badger to a wild bees' nest. The badger tears open the nest and roots out honey and grubs. The honeyguide bird is rewarded with the tasty wax honeycomb.

Many animals of the same kind groom and clean each other. Apes and monkeys tease out dirt and irritating insects like fleas from each other's fur. Often, the 'junior' animal will groom the 'senior' one.

Different kinds of animals may also help each other to keep clean. The Egyptian plover bird will pick leeches from a crocodile's skin, and will even hop inside its terrifying jaws to clean its teeth.

Little cleaner fish scurry right inside the mouth of the ferocious barracuda. They are perfectly safe, because the bigger fish seems to recognize them as helpers who will keep its mouth clean. The false cleaner fish is also safe from the barracuda. It looks exactly like the cleaner fish—but it does no cleaning!

Ants in an ant 'city' share out the jobs. Some look after the young. Some collect food, others build new tunnels, and a band of soldier ants defends the nest. Many ants keep insects called aphids, and eat the sweet sticky juice they make.

Enemies and Survival

For wild animals, life is a never-ending struggle against their enemies. Over millions of years, these animals have developed special ways to help them to survive.

Tortoises, crabs and shellfish wear tough armour-plating, and hedgehogs and porcupines bristle with sharp spines. Timid animals like deer and ostriches have long, strong legs for running away.

Some colours are a code for danger in the animal world. The black-and-yellow stripes of bees and wasps warn their enemies that they sting, while the brilliant red of the ladybird means it has an unpleasant taste. Some harmless animals have copied this clever means of defence. There are some flies which look exactly like wasps, but they have no stings!

The northern musk oxen shown below have great horns to defend themselves and their young. If hungry wolves attack, the oxen will form a circle facing outwards. No wolf can get through the ring of

horns to reach the young oxen sheltering safely in the centre.

Some animals spend a lot of time trying very hard to look like twigs or leaves. By blending into the background they can hide from their attackers and lie in wait for their own victims at the same time. This method of defence is called camouflage.

Polar bears living among snow and ice are white, and the tiger's stripes match the tall grass through which it silently stalks its prey. The ptarmigan bird and the stoat have coats which become white in winter, while the chameleon lizard can actually change its colour to match its background!

Fishes are in danger from the birds above them and other fish below them. So a fish will often have a dark upper side and a light-coloured belly. Seen from above, the dark colour blends with the colour of the sea. From below, its silvery belly is hard to see against the sunlight sparkling on the water.

Some of the best camouflage artists are insects. They can look like leaves, twigs, bark, and even flowers. These are:
1. Katydid mimicking lichen. 2. Purple thorn moth caterpillar pretending to be a twig. 3. Treble bar moth on tree bark.
4. Leaf bug. 5. Thorn tree hoppers looking like thorns. 6. Stick insect.

The caribou follow
fixed routes. They
cross lakes and rivers
and travel up to 160
kilometres a day. If
their food of lichen and
grass is buried
beneath the snow,
they paw at the
ground to uncover it.

Animal Journeys

Every winter in North America, herds of up to 20,000 caribou trek slowly southwards. They escape the deep snows to find food where it is warmer. In the spring, when the snow melts, they trail back north again.

Regular journeys like these are called migrations. The animals may travel thousands of kilometres, but nobody really knows how they find their way. Some may follow the sun or stars. Other animals may be guided by older ones who have made the journey before. Next time they go, they may recognize landmarks along the route. But we do not know how a young cuckoo, reared by foster-parents and only a few months old, can find its way to Africa all by itself.

Following the Sun

The champion long-distance traveller is a seabird called the Arctic tern. It migrates halfway around the world—from its breeding ground in the Arctic all the way to the Antarctic! That way, the tern can feast on the millions of insects that dance their way through the short summers at both poles. The rest of the year is spent on the wing. Yet this incredible round trip of 35,000 kilometres a year is mainly over seas without landmarks.

Swallow

Migration routes of swallows from Africa to Europe.

EUROPE

A bullfinch watches the swallows leave

Swallows are sun-loving birds which cover 20,000 kilometres a year to avoid winter altogether. In spring, they fly north to build their nests in Europe.

When the days grow cooler again, flocks of swallows gather to fly across the seas to Africa. Many tired birds will rest on ships, after being battered by winds and dazzled by lighthouses.

Some water creatures migrate, too. Freshwater eels make a remarkable ocean journey in order to lay their eggs. The tiny transparent baby eel hatches in the quiet waters of the Sargasso Sea, to the west of the Atlantic Ocean. For the next three years it gradually drifts across the sea. Eventually it swims up a European or North American river, where it stays for many years—until it returns to the Sargasso Sea again to mate.

Migration route of swallows from Europe to Africa.

AFRICA

A carmine bee-eater watches the swallows arrive

Bison wander the North American plains in search of grazing places, and African antelopes follow the rains to find the freshest grasslands. The migrating caribou are followed by packs of prowling wolves, who wait for a chance to pounce on any animal who might be rash enough to stray from the protection of the herd. In late summer, huge colourful clouds of monarch butterflies flutter south from North America to winter in Mexico.

Perhaps the strangest animal journey of all is the march of the lemmings. These little animals make their homes in cold northern countries, where they live in burrows in the ground. About every four years, the burrows become overcrowded and food is very scarce. When this happens, thousands of lemmings leave home on a journey from which they will never return. Many drown crossing rivers, or diving into the sea, in their unstoppable search for new land. Although most of these lemmings will die, it means that the ones that remain at home may live.

Bison

Antelope

38

Geese

Thousands of swans and geese fly from the Arctic in autumn. These birds arrive just as the swallows are leaving. Northern Europe in winter is too cold for swallows, but it is much warmer than the snowy Arctic where the ground, lakes and rivers become covered with ice.

Swallows

Caribou

Monarch butterflies

Wolf

Lemmings

The Winter Sleep

Winter causes problems for many animals. There is less food about, and small animals need to eat a lot to keep warm during the freezing weather. Some, like swallows, solve the problem by migrating to warmer countries. Many hunters like stoats and foxes stay awake in the bitter cold, but they often go hungry. Some animals give up the battle altogether and go to sleep.

This winter sleep is called hibernation. A dormouse builds a winter nest below ground or in a hollow tree stump. The little animal gradually stops eating. At last it drops into a deep sleep from which it will not stir until the warm days of spring.

Fish, reptiles like snakes and tortoises, and amphibians like frogs and toads are cold-blooded. This means they *have* to hibernate, as cold-blooded animals get their warmth from their surroundings. If the weather freezes, they freeze too.

Before hibernating, an animal eats a lot of food to make a store of fat in its body. During the winter sleep its body will use up this food. Bears which are fat when they hibernate are very thin when they awake in the spring.

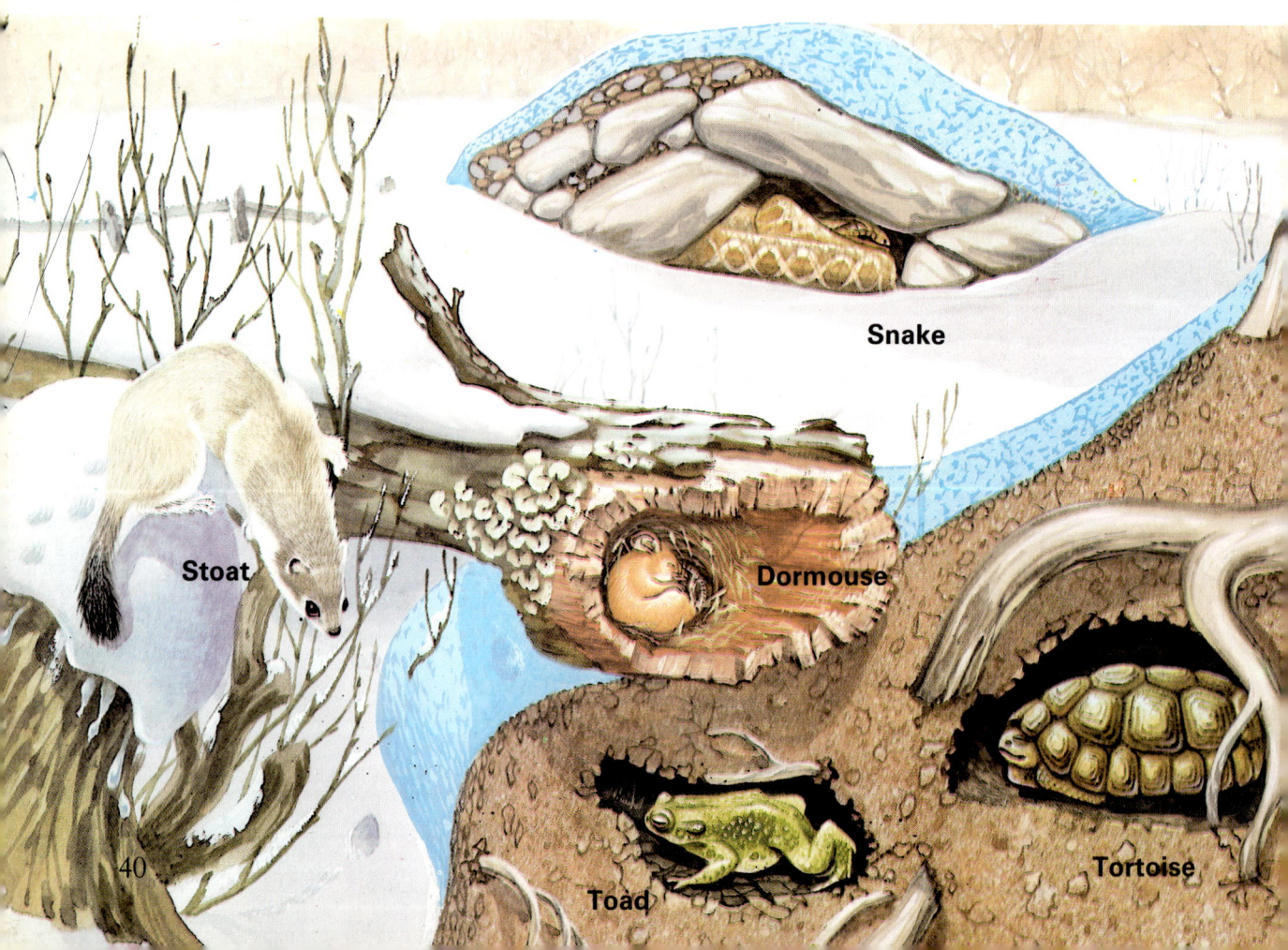

Snake

Stoat

Dormouse

Toad

Tortoise

A hibernating animal cools down as it sleeps. Its heartbeat slows down, and it takes fewer breaths. Frogs and underwater hibernators like terrapins actually stop breathing altogether. Dormice sleep so deeply that you cannot wake them, but squirrels, hedgehogs, badgers and bats often wake up on mild winter days to look for food. Squirrels make a store of nuts in the autumn for this reason. As soon as the weather begins to get cold again, they fall asleep once more.

Badger

Brown bear

Newt

Hedgehog

Tracks and Signs

In winter, when the ground is white with snow, it is easy to spot animals' footprints. They show up well in soft and muddy earth, too. These tracks are a useful clue as to what animals have been passing by.

Here are some mammals' tracks for you to spot. The ones you will probably see most often are those of pet cats and dogs.

Birds also leave tracks, but these are often harder to tell apart. However, the size of the print is a clue to the bird's size. And prints can

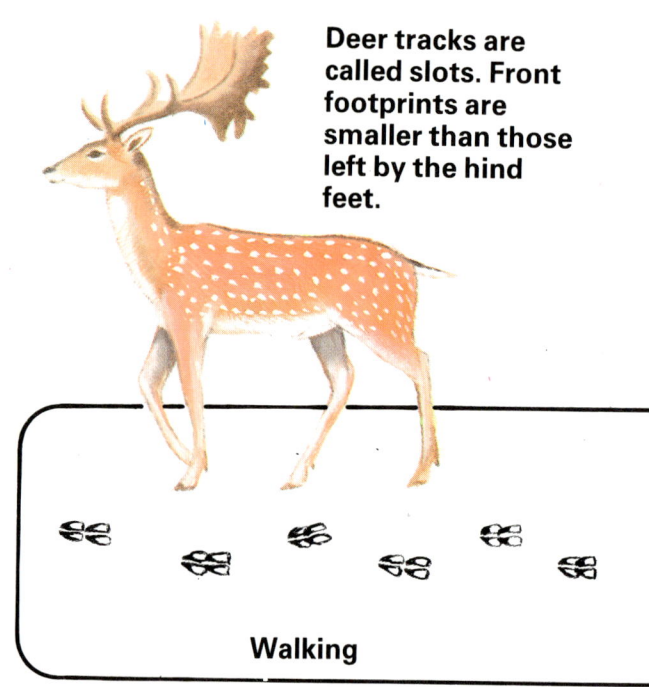

Deer tracks are called slots. Front footprints are smaller than those left by the hind feet.

Walking

Badger tracks show five toe marks and a long bar-shaped main pad.

Fox tracks show four round toes, the same size and shape as the main pad.

Dog tracks: four toes and a main pad which is triangular in shape.

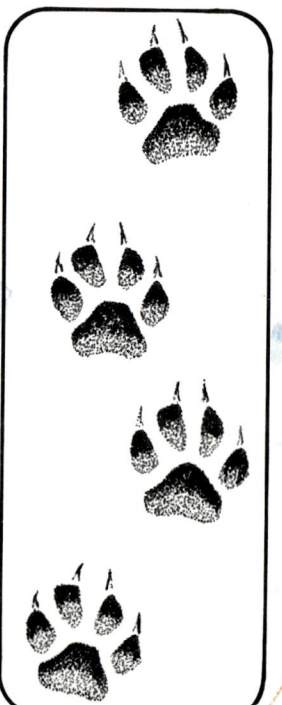

42

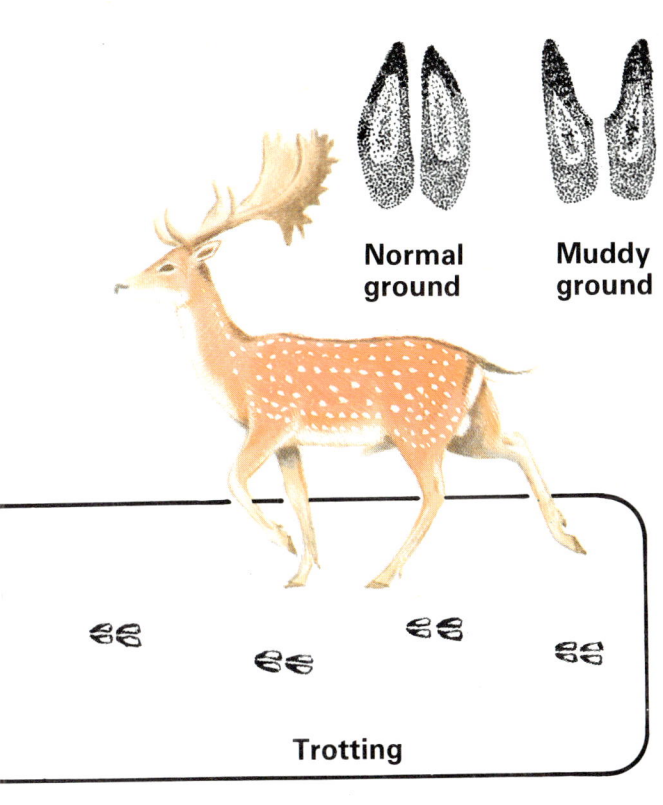

Normal ground   **Muddy ground**

Trotting

tell you if the bird was hopping (feet together, side by side) or walking (one foot in front of the other).

Animals leave many other signs, too. Squirrels and field mice nibble holes in nuts. House mice tear up paper for nests. Woodpeckers, deer and squirrels all rip strips of bark off trees. Playing otters often leave a slide on a snowy or muddy bank.

Droppings are another good clue. Rabbits leave piles of little round pellets. You may also be able to find an owl pellet. The owl swallows small animals and birds whole. Then it coughs up these little balls of bones, fur and feathers.

Cat tracks show four toes and an oval main pad. The claw marks do not show.

Rabbit tracks: front prints are small, hind prints long and side by side.

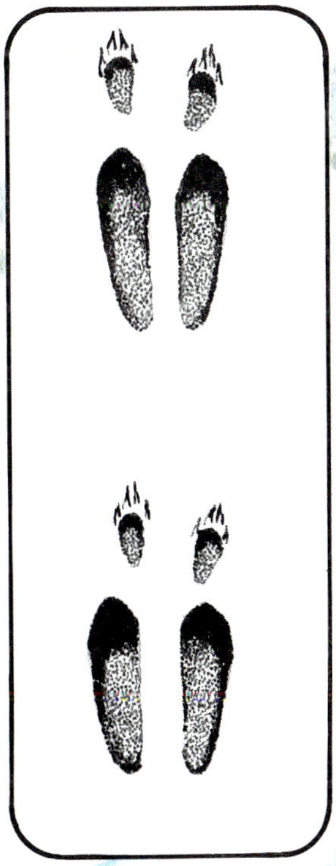

Otter tracks: called the 'seal'. Webs between five toe prints.

The Midnight World

When the hunting owl swoops overhead, tiny fieldmice tremble with fear. It will find them on even the darkest night. An owl can see very well in the dark, and can hear the tiniest rustle in the grass beneath.

The owl and other animals of the night have been sleeping all day. Now the sun is setting, and most animals are returning to their homes to sleep. But for the creatures of the night, the darkness is a signal for them to leave their beds in search of food.

The fields and woods are alive with animals at night. Fallow deer and rabbits graze on leaves, grass and berries. The nightjar hunts for moths, and the hedgehog looks for slugs and snails. But the hedgehog must be very careful. It may be eaten itself by the powerful badger—the only animal whose jaws and teeth are tough enough to tackle the hedgehog's prickles. The rabbit has to keep a sharp lookout for the badger, too—as well as the fox, the owl, the stoat and the polecat!

Night Visitors

If you watch quietly and patiently in your garden at night, you may be lucky enough to see animals prowling through the shadows. If you shine a torch around, you are bound to pick out many slugs, snails, moths and beetles.

Foxes were once a rare sight in towns, but during a very cold winter they may be seen raiding dustbins and stealing the scraps left out for birds.

Bats can often be seen swooping low over the garden. Bats are almost blind, but they have a special hearing system. They send out high-pitched sounds which bounce back from the objects in their path. Guided by these echoes, a bat can fly around in search of moths to eat without bumping into obstacles.

Moles burrow in search of worms, throwing up little mounds of earth as they go.

The rat and the hedgehog in the picture sniff with interest at the insects in their path. They are watched in turn by the cat. It has been dozing by the fire all day. Now it is awake and alert. It slips silently from the house to join the midnight world.

Index

*Page references refer
to main entries only.*